HERE
COMES
SNOOPY

Selected Cartoons from
Snoopy, Vol. 1
by CHARLES M. SCHULZ

A FAWCETT CREST BOOK
New York

HERE COMES SNOOPY

This book, prepared especially for Fawcett Books,
a unit of CBS Publications, the Consumer Publishing
Division of CBS Inc., comprises the first half of SNOOPY,
and is reprinted by arrangement with Holt, Rinehart
and Winston, Inc.

Printed in the United States of America

55   54   53   52   51   50

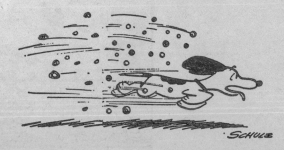

CLUMP!

YIPE!

REAL ALLIGATORS DON'T BITE THEIR OWN TONGUES...

EMPTY WATER DISH!

SCHULZ

PTUI!

SCHULZ

INDECISION IS AN AWFUL THING..

ZOOM!

NOW, YOU CUT THAT OUT!

SCHULZ

KLUNK! BUMP!BUMP!
bumpety-bump CRASH!!

WHAT IN THE WORLD WAS **THAT**?!

I GUESS IT WAS SNOOPY...IF HE DOESN'T LIKE HIS SUPPER, HE JUST PUSHES IT DOWNSTAIRS!

SCHULZ

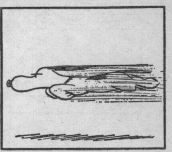

ZIP!

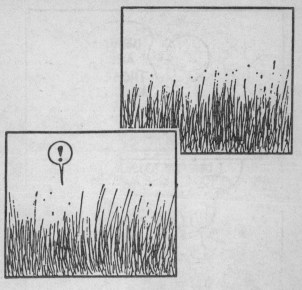

STOP IT! STOP IT THIS INSTANT! WITH ALL THE TROUBLE THERE IS IN THIS WORLD, YOU HAVE NO RIGHT TO BE SO HAPPY!!

SHE'S RIGHT... I'VE GOT TO START ACTING MORE SENSIBLE...

...TOMORROW!

SCHULZ

I THOUGHT I TOLD YOU TO STOP THAT DANCING?! YOU HAVE NO RIGHT TO BE SO HAPPY!!! NOW, STOP IT! DO YOU HEAR ME?!

SCHULZ

THERE SURE ARE A LOT OF WORMS ON THE SIDEWALK AFTER IT RAINS..

SCHULZ